MW01201416

Dear Single Girl

30 Days for Seeing Yourself and Your Singleness as Jesus Does

Jessica Faith Hagen

Lilies & Sparrows
Publishing

Lilies & Sparrows
Publishing

Cover and Interior Design by Jessica Hagen. Cover Photo by Kendall Lane on Unsplash.com.

Unless otherwise indicated, all Scripture quotations are taken from the *Holy Bible*, New Living Translation, copyright © 1996, 2004, 2015 by Tyndale House Foundation. Used by permission of Tyndale House Publishers, Inc., Carol Stream, Illinois 60188. All rights reserved.

Scripture quotations marked (NIV) are taken from THE HOLY BIBLE, NEW INTERNATIONAL VERSION®, NIV® Copyright © 1973, 1978, 1984, 2011 by Biblica, Inc.® Used by permission. All rights reserved worldwide.

Scripture quotations marked (AMP) are taken from the Amplified® Bible (AMP), Copyright © 2015 by The Lockman Foundation. Used by permission. www.lockman.org

Scripture quotations marked (CSB) are taken from The Christian Standard Bible. Copyright © 2017 by Holman Bible Publishers. Used by permission. Christian Standard Bible®, and CSB® are federally registered trademarks of Holman Bible Publishers, all rights reserved.

Scripture quotations marked (NKJV) are taken from the New King James Version®. Copyright © 1982 by Thomas Nelson. Used by permission. All rights reserved.

ISBN 978-0-9982353-3-2 (Paperback)
ISBN 978-0-9982353-4-9 (ebook)

Table of Contents

Hello and How to Use

Dear friend,

Would you believe me if I said I'm a little teary-eyed as I write these words to you?

That's because I'm just so overjoyed, humbled, and expectant that you're reading this.

I'm overjoyed that you're ready to ditch the lies about singleness and embrace this season as the true gift it is.

I'm humbled that you've chosen these words of mine to help you do that.

And I'm expectant that God is going to do a beautiful, powerful, transformational work in your heart.

When it comes to singleness, I haven't always had much joy or hope.

In my early twenties, I struggled with some deep discontentment in my singleness. I definitely DID NOT want to be single and was discouraged and disappointed that my dream for marriage had yet to be fulfilled.

If you would have told me then that at 29-almost-30, I would *still* be single, I probably would have cried.

If you would have also told me that at 29-almost-30, I would actually be okay with *still* being single, I probably would have laughed.

But deep in my heart, I would have also asked, *How?*

How would I come to have contentment in singleness, and overcome the lies and insecurities that made me so miserable about being single?

Maybe you're asking that, too.

Don't get me wrong, I still struggle with discontentment, discouragement, and doubts about my worth in singleness.

But they no longer define this season of my life. I've learned to live with joy, hope, and confidence.

How?

In a word: Jesus.

And that is my hope and prayer for you as you use this devotional: that you would encounter Jesus, experience His love, and embrace all the goodness He has for you, right here, right now.

Using this devotional is pretty straightforward: just sit down with this book, your Bible, a pen and journal - and maybe your favorite beverage and snack - and dive in with an open heart.

Now, before we begin, could I pray for you?

Dear Jesus,
We come to you with expectant hearts. I ask that you meet the one reading this right where she is, in whatever heartache, loneliness, and fears she may be feeling.

As she reads these words and reads Your Word, help her to see herself and her singleness as You do. Help her to know her worth in You. Fill her heart with hope and joy. Pour out Your love and kindness.

We thank You for Your presence and Your promise. Draw near to us as we draw near to You.

Amen.

Praying for you + cheering you on,
Jessica Faith

Part 1:

Your Singleness is a Gift

Day 1:
What Does Singleness Mean to You?

Single... what does that word mean to you?

Maybe it means being alone.
Maybe it represents unfulfilled dreams of marriage and family.
Maybe it stirs up questions about your worth and purpose.
Maybe it causes feelings of discontentment in this season.
Maybe it reminds you of attending weddings with no "plus one" and
that embarrassing bouquet toss and those awkward questions of
When will you get married? and *Why are you still single?*

But what if it doesn't have to be like that?

What if, in the midst of all the hard stuff, singleness could also mean
adventure and opportunity; growing in faith; friendships and
community; pursuing our dreams; using our gifts; becoming more
fully who God created us to be?

How?

In a word: Jesus.

Singleness doesn't have to be defined by loneliness or insecurities or
unmet longings or discontentment. In Christ, this word can take on
new meaning, and this season can hold real beauty, purpose, and joy.

I'm guessing that since you've picked up this devotional, there's at
least a part of you that's struggled with being single. I'm also
guessing that since you picked up this devotional, you're ready to
grab hold of that beauty, purpose, and joy.

It starts by starting right where you are and asking Jesus to meet you
there.

Jesus says, "I am the way, the truth, and the life." (Jn. 14:6)

Jesus says, "I am the vine; you are the branches. Those who remain in me, and I in them, will produce much fruit." (Jn. 15:5)

Jesus says, "I am the bread of life. Whoever comes to me will never be hungry again. Whoever believes in me will never be thirsty." (Jn. 6:35)

Over and over and over in Scripture, Jesus declares Himself to be the Source - the Source of joy, peace, comfort, truth, hope, confidence, security, wholeness, and all the goodness of life.

When it comes to knowing our worth, living with joy, and holding onto hope, are we looking for "the one", or are we looking to the One who created us for relationship with Him?

No matter our relationship status, we will never find fulfillment outside of a relationship with Jesus.

Friend, Jesus wants to meet you where you are - in your loneliness and longing, in your discouragement and disappointment, in your hopes and heartache.

Jesus wants to be your Source.

So, what if we were to define *single* in a new way? What if we were to see our singleness and see ourselves as Jesus does? What if we were to look to Jesus as our Source of worth, hope, and joy?

Well, get ready, 'cause that's exactly what we're going to do!

Read the seven "I Am" statements of Jesus: John 6:35, John 8:12, John 10:7, John 10:11, John 14:6, John 15:5.

What does *singleness* mean to you?

Which one of the seven "I Am" statements of Jesus spoke most to you? Consider writing it down and putting it somewhere you will see it often.

What would it look like for you to live with Jesus as your Source?

Day 2:
Your Singleness is a Gift

Your singleness is a gift.

Yep, you read that right!

Your singleness is a gift. But how often do we actually think of it as a gift? How often do we actually enjoy it, savor it, delight in it as a gift should be?

I think more often we see it as a season that's to be ended as soon as possible. We see it as only about waiting and preparing for marriage. We see it as less significant and purposeful and good than marriage.

1 Corinthians 7:25-40 is a passage of Scripture that talks a lot about singleness.

To be honest with you, I squirm a bit when I read this passage, because when it mentions singleness, it can sound as if God doesn't want me to be married. It can sound as if God wants me to stay single forever.

"I think it is best to remain as you are… a woman who is no longer married or has never been married can be devoted to the Lord and holy in body and in spirit." (vs. 26, 34)

These words were written by a single guy named Paul, and I kind of wish I could meet Paul and roll my eyes at him and say, *"You can't be serious."*

But when these verses are read in context, we learn that Paul isn't saying our relationship status makes us better Christians.

Paul was writing to a specific church in specific circumstances. He was giving advice and direction regarding questions widows, those engaged, and even parents of singles had about whether or not finding spouses should still be of utmost importance, especially for single women.

In his advice, Paul was really turning things upside down.

In a culture where a woman's purpose and place were seen to be in the home - married and having babies - Paul says there's nothing wrong with being single. That it can actually be *good* to be single.

Paul speaks of a purpose higher than marriage: devotion to the Lord. This should come first, this should be the goal, this should be the highest priority.

Paul's real message here is that whatever our relationship status is, we are to live wholeheartedly devoted to Jesus. And our decisions in seeking a relationship or staying single should come out of that devotion.

I've come to understand that when 1 Corinthians 7 talks about singleness, it isn't saying that God wants everyone to always be single.

Rather, it's saying that singleness is a gift - a time for cultivating wholehearted devotion to Jesus, a time for growing in faith and contentment and self-control, a time for seeking and building the Kingdom of God.

Yes, singleness is a gift, a gift just as beautiful, purposeful, and joyful as marriage.

Read 1 Corinthians 7:25-40.

According to this passage, what are some blessings of singleness?

What are some things you enjoy about being single?

What is one way you can cultivate devotion to the Lord in this season?

Day 3:
The Giver

Both singleness and marriage are gifts.

The thing about gifts is, they're *given*.

They aren't a paycheck we work for. They aren't a reward we earn. They're not even a prize we "like this post, follow this account, and tag three friends" in hopes of winning.

The other thing about gifts is, there is a *giver*.

In Matthew 7:11, Jesus describes God as a Father who gives good gifts to those who ask Him.

But maybe when it comes to marriage, we're wondering if God is holding out on us. I mean, I know I've asked, even begged, Him for a significant other.

In Luke 15, Jesus tells a story of a prodigal son. But really, the story is more about a very good Father.

After the younger son disrespectfully demands his inheritance early, squanders said inheritance, and returns home in hopes of becoming a hired hand, the father forgives his son and restores to him the rights of sonship - with a big party no less!

Talk about undeserved, unmerited, unearned goodness!

Meanwhile, the older son has stayed home and worked hard. Now, he's feeling miffed and cheated that his wayward brother is getting a party, while he has "been slaving for you and never disobeyed your orders. Yet you never gave me even a young goat so I could celebrate with my friends." (v. 29, NIV)

In a lot of ways, I can relate to the younger son. I've sinned grievously against my Father, but I've also experienced His amazing, saving grace.

And in a lot of ways, I can relate to the older son, saying to my Father, "I'm living for you, I'm doing what you want, so why am I not getting what I want? Why am I not being blessed with a cute and kind boyfriend? Is there some good Christian deed I still need to check off before I'm eligible to meet the one?"

Have you ever thought something like this?

In this thinking, we turn our relationship with the Father into rules we must follow.

Like the younger son, we're demanding what we think is ours to have. Like the older son, we're feeling cheated out of what we think we deserve to have.

Like both sons, we've elevated the gift above the Giver Himself.

But like the father in the story, our Heavenly Father says to us, "You are always with me, and everything I have is yours." (v. 31, NIV)

You are always with me. Our relationship with God comes first. This is the ultimate gift.

And everything I have is yours. Our Father does not withhold His goodness from us but gives generously to draw us closer to Himself.

This is worth celebrating!

Read Luke 15:11-32.

What do you learn about your Heavenly Father from this story?

Have you ever viewed marriage as something you must earn?

In what ways have you elevated the gifts above the Giver?

What would it look like for you to celebrate God's goodness to you?

Day 4:

Don't Let the Enemy Steal the Gift

We've learned that singleness is a gift - a joyful, beautiful, purposeful season to be lived in devotion to Jesus.

Well, there is a thief who will stop at nothing to rob of us of that gift. To steal the joy, kill the beauty, and destroy the purpose of this season. (See Jn. 10:13)

And the primary way this enemy works is through lies. (See Jn. 8:44 and 2 Cor. 11:14) Often the lies aren't obvious, disguised as our own negative self-talk.

Do any of these thoughts resonate with you?

I'm single because I'm not lovable.
I'll be happy once I'm married.
If I had a significant other, I would feel beautiful.
I'll stop having insecurities, anxiety, and depression once I'm married.
I'm behind all my friends who are dating and married.
I'm missing out on the best life.
If I had a spouse, I would finally feel complete.
I need to lose weight before I'll be attractive to guys.
*My life will **really** begin once I'm married.*

At the core of these thoughts is the lie that our significance - who we are and why we were created - is dependent on our relationship status rather than in being created for relationship with Jesus.

The enemy wants to deceive us about our significance as single women because he doesn't want us to live as who God created us to be as single women. He wants to hold us back from experiencing, enjoying, and engaging in the goodness and purpose God has for us *right now* in relationship with Him.

What we think about our singleness, and about ourselves as single women, matters. Because what we *think* will take root in our hearts, shape our beliefs, and mold our attitudes and actions.

If I think I won't be happy until I'm married, I probably won't fully enjoy life when I'm single.

If I think I'm single because I'm not lovable, I probably won't have much confidence as a single woman.

If I think having a significant other is what makes me beautiful, I probably won't have a healthy body image.

Romans 12:2 says, "Don't copy the behavior and customs of this world, but let God transform you into a new person by changing the way you think."

There's a whole world full of women basing their worth and fulfillment and purpose on their relationship status, on their successes and failures, on their appearance and popularity.

We don't have to follow this pattern. We can be transformed from insecure to confident, discouraged to hopeful, discontented to joyful.

It starts with our own hearts and minds being renewed by the Holy Spirit. It starts by changing the way we think to being rooted in truth.

Read Psalm 119:60, John 8:31-32, John 14:16-17 & 26, 1 Corinthians 2:10-16, 2 Timothy 3:14-17, and Hebrews 4:12.

What lies have you believed about singleness or about yourself as a single woman?

According to the above verses, how can you know the truth?

What's one step you can take to change your thinking and replace the lies with truth?

Day 5:
What If?

What if I never get married?

Have you ever had that thought?

What if I never get to plan a wedding?
What if I never get to experience the deep intimacy of marriage?
What if I never know the love of a husband?
What if I never have a spouse to make a home, raise a family, do life with?

The reality is, God doesn't promise you marriage.

Maybe that makes you uncomfortable. Maybe it makes you fearful. Maybe it even makes you a bit angry.

But here's another reality: Jesus is enough.

I don't say that lightly. I don't say that as a cliché. I don't say that to diminish your longings or make you feel ashamed for your desires.

I say it as a single woman who has wrestled with the *"what ifs"* and has had to fight hard to believe it's true.

Jesus is enough.

In the first devotion, we read the seven "I Am" statements of Jesus.

These statements made by Christ are tied to the name of God. It is the name He told Moses to speak to the Israelites when they asked who had sent him to lead them out of slavery in Egypt: *I AM WHO I AM* (Ex. 3:14).

In declaring this name, God declares He is self-existent, and all life and breath come from Him. He declares He is eternal and unchanging, and so will always be good to His people and faithful to His promises. He declares He lacks for nothing and is all-sufficient for everything.

Jesus declares, *I AM.* (Jn. 8:58)

You see, Jesus not only wants to be our Source, but our Sufficiency. Our life and breath. Our fulfillment. Our enough.

Believing Jesus is enough doesn't mean we can't long for marriage or hope for a spouse to do life with.

But it does mean we don't look to those things as our ultimate fulfillment. It means we know that even if we never get married, we still have enough. Enough love and intimacy, enough affection and delight, enough comfort and tenderness.

What if you never get married?

Do you believe you can still be fulfilled? Do you believe God is still good? Do you believe Jesus is worth it? Do you believe He is enough?

I know those *"what ifs"* are hard.

It's okay to wrestle with them.

Friend, Jesus wants to meet you here. Sit in His presence and let Him reveal Himself to you.

I'm confident you're going to win the wrestling match, because you have a fierce Love on your side, who will show Himself to be... *enough.*

Let's re-read the "I Am" statements of Jesus: John 6:35, John 8:12, John 10:7, John 10:11, John 14:6, John 15:5.

Who does Jesus declare Himself to be in each one?

What *"what if"* questions do you have? Bring them before God. Wrestle with them.

What would it look like for you to live with Jesus as your Source *and* Sufficiency?

Day 6:
More Than In the Meantime

We often talk about singleness as a season. I've already referred to it as a season multiple times in this devotional.

We do live in seasons, but we're not living for a season, whether that season is dating or college or marriage or career or having kids or empty nesting or retirement.

We're living for eternity.

Ecclesiastes 3 speaks about seasons and eternity, and verse 11 says, "He has made everything beautiful *and* appropriate in its time. He has also planted eternity [a sense of divine purpose] in the human heart [a mysterious longing which nothing under the sun can satisfy, except God]." (AMP)

It may seem like this season of singleness doesn't matter. Like it's just a holding pattern until our real purpose begins with marriage.

This idea can cause us to live an "in the meantime" life.

I know I've said something like this: "I want to be married, but I'm not, so in the meantime I'm just…"

In the meantime, I'm just doing these things to kill this time until I meet the right one and my life can really begin.

This implies that singleness is less purposeful than marriage. That we as single women are less significant than those in a relationship.

When the seasons first began, God established our purpose and significance:

"So God created human beings in his own image.
   In the image of God he created them;
      male and female he created them." Gen. 1:27

This is why we were created and who we were created to be: *in His image*.

Being created in the image of God means first that we are created for relationship with God.

God is Trinity: Father, Son, and Holy Spirit, in perfect communion with Himself.

And God created us in love to enter into communion with Him.

Being created in the image of God also means we are created to reflect His character in our relationships with others.

As we live in relationship with God, He grows us in Christ-likeness. Our lives are to point to the presence of the One true God and be a testimony of the Gospel of Christ and His work in our lives.

This sounds like more than "in the meantime". This sounds like purpose for now, and forever.

How we live out this purpose may look different in different seasons, but the purpose remains the same: know God and make Him known.

Your singleness is not meant to be lived as "in the meantime". Your singleness is meant to be lived with purpose and meaning. Because you have purpose and meaning that go way beyond a season, and way beyond a relationship status.

Read Matthew 28:19-20, 2 Corinthians 5:17-21, Ephesians 1:4-6, and 1 Peter 4:10-11.

What do these verses say about our purpose?

In what ways are you living "in the meantime"?

How can you pursue more purposeful living right now?

Part 2:

Your

Dreams,

God's Plan

Day 7:
When?

I remember sitting around a bonfire with some of my single friends, each sharing what was hardest for us about being single. One thing many said was hardest for them was not knowing when singleness would end. We all agreed if we just knew *when* we would get married (preferably before 30), we would have a much easier time being content in our singleness.

While we all saw so much good in our lives, that unknown was getting in the way of enjoying the good. It was causing a lot of fear about the future, namely FOMO: fear of missing out.

In not knowing *when* we will get married, we're left uncertain *if* we will get married, and fearing that maybe we're missing out on something better.

Unknowns are hard. Unknowns are scary. Unknowns are… well, unknown.

Omniscient is a word used to describe God.

This is a fancy word that means God is *all-knowing*. There is nothing He doesn't know. There is no unknown for Him. He doesn't have to ask *When?* or *What if?* or *How?*

Jeremiah 29:11 gives us this promise about something God knows:

"'For I know the plans I have for you' - this is the Lord's declaration - 'plans for your well-being, not for disaster, to give you a future and a hope.'" (CSB)

God knows His plans for us. He knows the answer to that *When?* And the best part? His plans for us are the *best* plans for us.

Psalm 139:1 says there's something else God knows:

"O Lord, you have examined my heart and know everything about me."

God knows YOU!

He knows your dreams. He knows your questions. He knows your fears. He knows the hard stuff you're facing. He knows your pet peeves. He knows all those little things that make you smile. He knows your past. He knows what you need. He knows (and gets!) your sense of humor. He knows your favorite food and color and book and song. He knows your tears. He knows your weaknesses. He knows your strengths.

Maybe the thought of someone knowing you inside and out causes a knot in your stomach.

The knowledge God has of you isn't just facts, two columns of pros and cons, a flat profile. It is relational knowing, as the One who specifically and intricately formed you as you.

When it comes to the *Whens* and *Hows* and *What ifs* of singleness, we don't have to have FOMO.

Rather, we can "know with great confidence that God, who is deeply concerned about us, causes all things to work together as a plan for good." (Rom. 8:28, AMP)

Read Psalm 139.

According to this passage, what does God know about you?

How do you feel knowing that God fully knows you?

How can you shift to thinking about your future with hope instead of worry and fear?

Day 8:
Pinterest Plans

Confession: I have a secret Pinterest board with ideas for my dream wedding. I also have a Pinterest board called "Dream Home." And one that shows my dream wardrobe.

As seen in these collections of pictures and ideas, I love dreaming.

When I was growing up, I would often daydream about my future as a grown-up.

I would think about the seasons to come, mapping them out in my head to create a perfect plan.

And of course, a big part of that plan was to date, fall in love with, and marry a godly man.

But as I'm sure you know, life doesn't always go according to our plans.

Making plans is one way we try to deal with those unknowns. It's one way we try to answer the *When?* It's one way we try to ensure our life turns out how we dreamed it would.

There's nothing wrong with making plans, setting goals, and pursuing dreams.

But how tightly are we holding onto them? Are we clenching them with closed fists, or are we holding them with open hands to God?

In Ephesians 3, Paul prays for those reading his letter, and he ends his prayer with this praise to God:

"Now to him who is able to do immeasurably more than all we ask or imagine, according to his power that is at work within us, to him be glory in the church and in Christ Jesus throughout all generations, for ever and ever! Amen." (vv. 20-21, NIV)

I really like how the Amplified version phrases verse 20:

"Now to Him who is able to [carry out His purpose and] do superabundantly more than all that we dare ask or think [infinitely beyond our greatest prayers, hopes, or dreams], according to His power that is at work within us."

immeasurably more... infinitely beyond...

Do we believe this?

Or are we afraid that if we open our hands, letting go of those Pinterest-perfect plans, we'll be giving up on our dreams and settling for second best?

God is second best to none.

His dreams for us are so much bigger and better than our dreams for ourselves.

Trusting God means submitting to Him. It means giving Him our dreams, not so He can take them away and smash them to ground, but so He can shape them and mold them to reflect His plans for us.

In our planning and dreaming, are we leaving room for God?

No, that's not right...

Because God doesn't just want a *room;* He wants the *whole house.*

He doesn't just want a Pinterest board; He wants all the plans. He doesn't just want your dreams; He wants your heart.

What dreams do you have?

Describe a time God did more than you had asked or imagined.

Spend some time reading and praying Ephesians 3:14-21 for yourself.

Day 9:
What Are You Waiting For?

For you, has being single ever felt like just a bunch of waiting around?

Like Rapunzel in the tower, Snow White and Sleeping Beauty in their enchanted slumbers, Cinderella in the cinders, we're waiting for Prince Charming to come along and rescue us from loneliness, boredom, insecurities, disappointments, and give us "true love's kiss" and the "happily ever after" we've been longing for.

The phrase "wait on the Lord" is one I've heard a lot regarding singleness, especially in connection to trusting God's timing.

But what does this phrase actually mean?

When I think of waiting, I think of standing in line waiting for my turn. I think of sitting in a waiting room until my name is called. I think of sending a text and then waiting for a reply.

Waiting is usually associated with monotony, delayed gratification, impatience, and frustration. We typically don't like to be told to wait.

Yet in singleness, it can seem like "wait" is all we're hearing, and waiting is all we're doing.

I think sometimes we confuse "wait on the Lord" with "wait for marriage".

We treat our singleness like it's waiting room: waiting to pursue that dream, do that hard thing, go after that goal, take that step of faith.

We think, *I can't do that without a spouse by my side.* We think, *Someday, when I'm married...*

When we see the phrase "wait on the Lord" in Scripture, the word "wait" often comes from the Hebrew word *qavah*. This word stresses focusing the mind in a certain direction with an expectant attitude. It is looking forward with assurance.

Waiting on the Lord means believing and being assured that God will be who He says He will be and will do what He says He will do no matter how impossible it seems at the moment.

Because He will.

This definition of waiting doesn't conjure up images of long lines and waiting rooms. Rather, it gives a picture of hope and expectancy and defying the odds.

When was the last time we felt that way about our singleness? When was the last time we saw waiting not as a delaying of our dreams, but as anticipation that God is going to show up in a bigger-than-we-could-ever-imagine way?

Waiting on the Lord doesn't mean we're waiting to live, to pursue our dreams, go on dates, travel somewhere new, buy a house.

It doesn't mean we have to wait for Prince Charming to come and rescue us so we can live happily ever after.

Because our Rescuer has already come!

We've already been set free from captivity, awakened from dark slumber, lifted from the ashes, and given the happiest of happily ever afters by the truest of true loves.

So what are we waiting for?

Read Psalm 27:13-14, Psalm 33:20-22, and Psalm 130.

According to these verses, what is promised for those who wait on the Lord?

In what ways have you treated singleness like a "waiting room"?

How would waiting on the Lord look different than waiting for marriage?

Day 10:
Keep Dreaming

I remember when I got my first gray hair. I was 25.

At first, it was no big deal; I just plucked it out. But it wasn't long after that I found a few more, and I just wasn't sure how to feel about it.

It wasn't the gray hairs themselves that bothered me so much as the fact that I was getting older, yet still wasn't married. Time was passing, but that wedding day I dreamed of didn't seem to be getting any closer.

I had dreams of growing old, going gray with someone, but what if I grew old alone?

I had dreams of raising kids with someone, but what if I reached an age when I couldn't have children anymore?

When year after year, birthday after birthday, goes by without our dreams coming true, it can seem less and less possible for them to come true, and it can be harder and harder to keep dreaming.

Disappointment can be a familiar feeling in our singleness and, if we let it, disappointment can become the narrative of our story, causing discouragement and despair.

But disappointment doesn't have to tell our story.

Rather, our story can be one of hope - hope that keeps us dreaming, even as birthdays come and go, gray hairs are found on our heads, and life turns out differently than we expected.

One of my favorite Scriptures about hope is found in Lamentations, which is ironic since the book of Lamentations is a lament.

It was written after the destruction of Jerusalem, sometime during the Israelites' exile in Babylon.

Yet tucked into chapter 3 are these words: "Yet I still dare to hope when I remember this..." (v. 21)

Even after the destruction, loss, grief, pain, and heartache, there was still hope stirring in the heart.

How was that possible?

Because they remembered this:

"The faithful love of the Lord never ends! His mercies never cease. Great is his faithfulness; his mercies begin afresh each morning. I say to myself, 'The Lord is my inheritance; therefore, I will hope in him!'" (vv. 22-24)

All our dreams may not come true, but each morning is the start of a new day in which we experience the promises of God to us coming true.

Friend, this is your reminder to keep dreaming.

Even when the waiting is long and hard. Even when you're discouraged and disappointed. Even when your life doesn't go as expected. Even when your dreams seem less and less possible. Even when your dreams don't come true.

This is your reminder to hold on to hope, because our hope is in Jesus, and He won't disappoint!

Read Lamentations 3:19-33

What are some of God's promises found in this passage?

Look back at those dreams you listed on Day 8. How do you feel about these dreams (i.e. hopeful, discouraged, frustrated, sad, etc.)?

How does placing your hope in Jesus give you hope for your dreams?

Day 11:
Praying for Your Dreams

Have you prayed about your singleness? Have you talked to God about your desire for a relationship? Have you spoken to Him about the dreams in your heart?

Maybe you've heard all the advice about singleness that emphasizes praying for your future spouse while contentedly waiting on God to bring you together.

But maybe those prayers haven't been answered, and you're feeling disillusioned and disappointed, longing for advice more practical than "Just pray, just trust, just be content."

Because often, there's no "just" about it. Often, faith feels hard, the wait feels long, and prayer feels messy.

Or maybe, you're afraid to pray for your dreams, asking God for opportunities to meet other single Christians and go on dates and have fun. Because that would mean you're desperate. That would mean you're not really trusting God's timing and will. That would mean you've made marriage into an idol.

When we find ourselves in either of these places - discouraged our prayers aren't being answered, or afraid to pray for the desires of our hearts - we need to remember what prayer is truly about: relationship with God.

Relationships take communication, and that's what prayer is: communicating with God.

And it is more. It is *communion* with God. It is a vulnerable act of trust, an intimate act of baring your soul before Jesus, laying it all out there for Him to see, to hold, to know, to shape.

Prayer is a way we give what is on our hearts to God, and it doesn't matter how broken the words, how imperfect the faith, how messy the emotions may be.

Psalm 66:20 says, "Praise God, who did not ignore my prayer or withdraw his unfailing love from me."

The beautiful thing about prayer is that not only can we pour out our hearts to God, but we can know that God will respond to our heart's cry, meeting us where we're at, providing what we truly need, and ultimately revealing Himself to us.

Maybe today the next step in becoming content, in trusting God, in finding hope in your singleness, is to pray.

Whether you're discouraged about your prayers for marriage not being answered, or you're afraid to pray for your desires because that might not be "spiritual" enough, Jesus wants to meet you where you're at.

I believe as you pray with a heart open to Him, He will speak to your heart and draw you closer to His heart.

Read Psalm 116:1-2

What promises are given in these verses?

What have been your thoughts and feelings when it comes
to praying for your dreams?

Spend some time praying right now. Then listen. What is
God speaking to your heart?

Day 12:
Your Dreams, God's Heart

When I was a little girl, I wanted to be a ballerina when I grew up. But for some reason, I never took ballet lessons. I did, however, take piano lessons, so there was a period of time when I wanted to be a piano teacher when I grew up. That soon changed to wanting to be fashion designer, but somewhere along the way, that dream faded, too.

One thing I've always dreamed of being?

A wife.

I've held this desire in my heart with hope for as long as I can remember. I've dreamed of making a home with someone and doing life together for God's glory. I've prayed that God would make this happen. I've waited on His timing and will.

But here I am: still single.

Still waiting. Still praying. Still hoping. Still dreaming.

And in the midst of all these stills, I can find myself wondering, does God really have a plan for me?

We read in Jeremiah 29:11, "'For I know the plans I have for you' - this is the Lord's declaration - 'plans for your well-being, not for disaster, to give you a future and a hope.'" (CSB)

If God knows His plans, if they're for our good, if He hears our prayers, if He promises joy and peace and security, then why…?

Why aren't my hopes and prayers being answered?
Why is she getting her dream while I'm still waiting for mine?

Why aren't doors opening and things falling into place?
Why do I feel like I'm left out of the Happily Ever After Club?

Jeremiah 29 goes on to say, "'In those days when you pray, I will listen. If you look for me wholeheartedly, you will find me. I will be found by you,' says the Lord." (vv. 12-14)

This is really what our hopes and dreams are all about: seeking the Lord with our whole heart, drawing closer and closer to the heart of God, pursuing our passions as an overflowing of pursuing Jesus.

We can trust God's plan for us because we can trust God's heart for us, because God's heart is for us.

We can know God's plan is good because God Himself is good.

We can know God's plan is full of hope because God Himself is our hope.

We can know God's plan is the best because God loves us (and all those around us) too much to make a plan that is anything less.

No, things may not turn out how we dreamed or expected.

But God doesn't disappoint those who hope and trust in Him, those who are after His heart.

Isn't that the best happily ever after a girl could dream up?

Read Jeremiah 32:38-41.

What do you learn of God's heart for people in these verses?

Are there any words or phrases that spoke to your heart?

In what ways have you drawn closer to God in your singleness? In what ways would you like to draw closer to Him in your singleness?

Part 3:
Loved

Day 13:

What's Wrong with Me?

I was sitting at a table, listening to the conversation around me, when they came up and made a show of looking at my left hand.

Seeing there was still no ring on it, they made a face of lighthearted shock, commented something about me not having a boyfriend, and then asked, "What's wrong with you?"

I have to note: I know they weren't saying it to be mean or demeaning.

But I still had to rapidly blink to keep back the tears. I still had to step into the bathroom as soon as I could to let those tears fall.

Has anything like this ever happened to you?

Has anything ever made you feel like there must be something wrong with you, like you're just not pretty enough, attractive enough, confident enough, smart enough, good enough because you're single?

Here's the thing: what's wrong with me and you is really the same thing that's wrong with all of us: sin.

Romans 3:23 makes it clear: "For all have sinned and fall short of the glory of God." (NIV)

Sin is anything we do that is disobedient to God. It's any thoughts or actions or words or attitudes or desires that go against God's character and will. So, sin causes separation between us and God.

And this sin and separation has consequences: "For the wages of sin is death..." (Rom. 6:23)

The biblical word for "good enough" is righteous.

Romans 3:10 says, "There is no one righteous, not even one."

Because of sin, we're not good enough. On our own, we are broken and fallen and insecure and unworthy and incomplete. On our own, we are deserving of punishment and death.

And a significant other won't make us good enough.

Because the issue isn't singleness; the issue is sin.

So our real need isn't a ring, but a Redeemer.

2 Corinthians 5:21 says, "God made Him who had no sin to be sin for us, so that in Him we might become the righteousness of God."

Jesus took care of our sin when He took our sin upon Himself and died the death we deserve. He took what makes us not good enough, and in exchange gives us *His* righteousness. He rescues us from a place of separation and brings us into right-standing with God.

Through Jesus, sin is broken, the broken is mended, and relationship with God is restored.

This is what makes us good enough.

So, we don't need a ring to prove there is nothing wrong with us, because we are clothed in Jesus' righteousness, and that is enough.

Read Romans 3:22-24, 2 Corinthians 5:17-21, Philippians 3:7-9, Titus 3:3-7, 1 Peter 2:24-25.

According to these verses, what makes you righteous (or good enough)?

How does this change how you see singleness and yourself as a single woman?

Have you repented of your sin and trusted in Jesus as your Lord and Savior?

Day 14:

Marrying Mr. Darcy

One time I played a game called *Marrying Mr. Darcy* with some friends.

If you're a fan of the author Jane Austen, you'll know who Mr. Darcy is, and why marrying him would be the goal of the game.

The basic premise of the game is that each player chooses one female character from Jane Austen's novel *Pride and Prejudice* and tries to earn points in such areas as wit, charm, and beauty, so they will become eligible for a proposal from one of the male characters, and *not* end up as an old maid.

I had a lot fun of playing (and won the game!), but it got me thinking: how often do I treat my own life like it's this game, tallying points to tally my worth and determine if I'm "eligible" to really be loved?

Having a good hair day: +5 points
Read my bible, said my prayers, served at church: +10 points
Instagram posts aren't as cute as So-and-So's: -15 points
Gained some weight: -10 points
Still single: -100 points

Maybe we don't actually keep a running score in our heads, but how many of us measure our worth based on things like these?

How many of us single gals measure our worth by our relationship status, believing since we're single, it must mean we are less worthy of love than those in a relationship?

One of my favorite passages that reminds me where my worth is really found is Ephesians, chapter 1, verses 4-7:

"Even before He made the world, God loved us and chose us in Christ to be holy and without fault in His eyes. God decided in advance to adopt us into His own family by bringing us to Himself through Jesus Christ. This is what He wanted to do, and it gave Him great pleasure. So we praise God for the glorious grace He has poured out on us who belong to His dear Son. He is so rich in kindness and grace that He purchased our freedom with the blood of His Son and forgave our sins."

Notice it says *before He made the world*. Before we did anything, God did everything. He gave us breath, He gave us worth, He gave us purpose, He gave us hope.

We have worth not because of what our relationship status says, but because God loves us, chose us, and sent His Son for us so that we could have relationship with Him.

Read Ephesians 3:3-8.

From this passage, list all the things God has done for you.

What things have you based your worth upon?

How does knowing you already have worth through what God has done for you change how you see yourself and your singleness?

Day 15:

Conversations that Leave Me Feeling Bleh

Person: Are you married? Dating anyone?

Me: No.

Person: No? Well, we'll have to fix that!

This is a conversation I've had in some form or another at various times since entering my 20s.

Maybe you've had conversations like that as well.

I don't know how they make you feel, but they tend to leave me feeling *bleh*.

It bothers me that in a few short sentences, I go from simply being single, to my singleness being a problem that needs to be solved, a brokenness that needs to be fixed.

Those with whom I have had these conversations are always speaking kindly. I believe many of them genuinely want to help.

It bothers me more when it's coming from someone who doesn't really know me and is just assuming I need a boyfriend to be happy and complete.

It bothers me more when the conversation just ends there, instead of showing interest in my life beyond my relationship status.

But the real reason conversations like this bother me and leave me feeling *bleh*, is that they stir up the insecurities in my heart.

The insecurities that say I *do* need a boyfriend to be happy and complete.

The insecurities that say I *don't* have identity and significance beyond my relationship status.

The insecurities that say I'm not pretty, or attractive, or likable, or lovable.

The insecurities that say I'm too much of this and not enough of that.

Friend, what insecurities stir in your heart?

Here's the thing: going on dates, having a significant other, and getting married won't make the insecurities go away.

It may cover them up for a bit. It may quiet them for a time. It may loosen their grip for a moment.

But it won't heal them.

That's a lot of pressure to put on another human. There is no person whose love, care, and respect can make us complete and whole.

Except the person of Jesus Christ.

Yesterday, we talked about how we have worth because we were created for relationship with God. Well, we are whole only when we live in that relationship through faith in Jesus.

Colossians 2:10 says, "So you also are complete through your union with Christ."

Our insecurities won't go away by striving for acceptance from other people. They will be healed as we place our confidence in Christ, believing we are who He says we are, and becoming the women He created us to be.

Are you defining yourself by your relationship status, or by your identity in Christ? Are you believing a relationship is the fix-it solution to your insecurities?

There is a relationship that brings healing and wholeness: our relationship with Jesus.

Read 2 Corinthians 5:17, Ephesians 2:10, Ephesians 5:8, Colossians 2:13, Colossians 3:12.

What insecurities do you have in your singleness?

Have you ever viewed a relationship as the solution to making those insecurities go away?

Who do the above verses say you are in Christ? How do they speak to your insecurities?

How can you look to Jesus for your wholeness and healing from insecurities?

Day 16:
Single But Not Alone

My biggest fear is being alone.

Not as in being by myself with no other people around. But as in having no place of belonging, where I'm accepted as who I am and the real me fits right in and I pour into others as they pour into me.

Because of this fear, the hardest part of singleness for me is dealing with loneliness: the wanting to share my life with someone, to walk through the hard and happy stuff together, to have "my person."

Maybe in your singleness, you're dealing with some loneliness, too.

I believe our loneliness is our soul's longing for belonging.

And I believe we have this longing because we were created to belong. We weren't created to do life alone, but to have relationships in which we do life together.

In Genesis 2, after God created the heavens and the earth and breathed life into man, there was one thing God said wasn't good: "It is not good for the man to be alone. I will make a helper suitable for him." (v. 18, NIV)

In creating woman to have relationship with man, God established relationships - community, family, friendships, marriage - as a part of His design for His creation.

We were created for relationship with God, but creation wasn't yet complete until there was a way for us to reflect His Image in relationship with others.

So, this longing for belonging isn't a bad thing.

But in our loneliness, we need to remember there is only One who can truly meet our longings for belonging and connection.

One of my favorite Bible verses is Zephaniah 3:17: "For the Lord your God is living among you. He is a mighty savior. He will take delight in you with gladness. With his love, he will calm all your fears. He will rejoice over you with joyful songs."

This verse tells us God is not only with us, but He *wants* to be with us - to save us, to delight in us, to be gladdened by us, to rejoice over us, to love us.

He wants to have a relationship with us in which He is not only our Savior, but also our Lord, our Friend, our Love.

This promise that God is always with us, never leaving or forsaking us, doesn't mean we won't ever experience loneliness.

But because of this promise, our loneliness can become space in which we lean deeper into Jesus. It can motivate us to pursue closer connection with Him. It can remind us that our belonging is found *first* in relationship with Him. And it can inspire us to build relationships with others that invite them into this belonging as well.

Read Isaiah 43:1-7.

List the promises in these verses.

When do you most feel lonely?

How do you feel knowing God is not only with you, but *wants* to be with you?

How could you shift your view of loneliness so that you see it as described in the last paragraph?

Day 17:
Remembered

The months leading up to my 25th birthday were hard.

With an unexpected loss in the family, heightened anxiety, feeling purposeless, and still discontent in my singleness, I was going through a bit of a quarter-life crisis, and was actually kind of dreading turning 25.

So imagine my surprise and joy when I walked into the room expecting a small dinner with my family, and several of my friends appeared from their hiding places, with gifts and balloons and apple pie.

My family had planned a little surprise to brighten my birthday and encourage my heart.

In that moment, I felt seen, valued, and understood.

It's a contrast to how we can so often feel in singleness: overlooked, forgotten, and left out.

Does God hear my prayers for a husband? Does He see my tears? Does He understand my longing for love and intimacy? Has He forgotten about me, about His plans for me, about my hopes and dreams?

One of my favorite stories in Scripture is found in 1 Samuel, chapter 1, and is about a woman named Hannah. Hannah was the mother of Samuel, who became the first prophet of Israel.

But before Hannah had Samuel, she went through many years of infertility.

One reason this is one of my favorite stories is that I can relate to Hannah. Yes, Hannah was married, but I still think she would understand the sadness and frustration of unmet longings, unfulfilled dreams, and unanswered prayers that so many (if not all) of us experience.

Another reason it's one of my favorite stories is found in verse 19, where it says, "… and the Lord remembered her." (NIV)

When Scripture says God remembers something, it's not saying He forgot, and then something jogged His memory, and now He remembers again.

The "remembered" in this verse comes from the Hebrew word *zakar*. This word speaks of remembering in such a way as to *never* forget. It is to mark or record, to retain in thought, to be mindful and to think on.

God never forgot Hannah.

And He never forgets you or me.

Even when we're lonely, even when we feel overlooked by others, even when we pray and pray and pray and aren't getting an answer, even when God seems distant, we are retained in His thoughts and recorded in His heart.

We are not overlooked. God sees us.
He sees *your* struggles, *your* joys, *your* hopes.

We are not ignored. God hears us.
He hears *your* prayers, *your* cries, *your* laughter.

We are not forgotten. God remembers us.
He remembers *your* dreams, *your* purpose, and who *you* are in Him.

Read 1 Samuel 1:1-28.

What do you learn about God from this passage?

How have you felt overlooked, forgotten, or left out in your singleness?

How does Hannah's story and the truth that God remembers you encourage your heart?

Day 18:
Loved

Once when I was scrolling on Instagram, I stopped at a picture of an adorable baby girl. It was a joyful announcement of the newborn's arrival into the world. It also announced the newborn's new name: Eleanore.

There was a little lurch in my heart as I read her name because that's the name I've always dreamed of giving my someday-daughter.

Now, I know I can still use the name Eleanore. But there was just something about knowing that new mom was naming her new daughter Eleanore that caused a bit of a sting.

That's my dream.
Yet it's not happening for me.
But it is for her.

Having unfulfilled dreams and unmet longings can be hard… especially as we see yet another engagement announcement, attend yet another wedding (and with no plus one), find out yet another friend is expecting.

In those situations, it's easy to ask deep in our hearts, *"Why her and not me? Could God perhaps, maybe, possibly love her more?"*

In those situations, it's easy to equate singleness or marriage, fulfillment of dreams or still waiting for dreams, as the degree of God's love for us, believing those are the ultimate signs of our "lovableness".

But that's just not how God works. That's just not who God is.

1 John 4:8 tells us, "God is love."

God. Is. Love.

Can we just let that sink in for a moment?

Love is part of God's character, and since God is unchanging, His love is unchanging. Since God is infinite, His love is infinite. It's not given in degrees of *more* or *less*, depending on us deserving it or earning it.

God loves us, not because of anything we've done, not because we've earned it, not because we're perfect, but because *God is love.*

Friend, you are so, so, so loved.

Can we let that sink in for a moment as well?

You - right here, right now - are loved wholly, tenderly, passionately by God. You are loved by God who created you to have relationship with Him. You are loved by God who sent His Son to redeem you from sin. You are loved by God to whom you can say, "I love You, too."

I can't answer why some seem to get their dreams right away while others wait.

But I do know this: Jesus is the only One who can truly satisfy our deepest longings for love and intimacy and connection.

In Him we find fulfillment, wholeness, and... perfect love.

Read Psalm 86:5, Isaiah 54:10, Jeremiah 31:3, Romans 8:38-39, 1 John 3:1.

What words are used to describe God's love?

When was a time you saw someone else getting the thing you were dreaming of and waiting for? How did you feel about them, about yourself, about God?

How does knowing God's love for you change your view?

What's one way you can rest in God's love for you?

Part 4:
Love Your Single Life

Day 19:
When Singleness is Stealing Your Joy

Have you ever felt like singleness is stealing your joy?

I have.

In my early twenties, my singleness was a sore spot of discontentment in my heart, and I thought being in a relationship would bring a happiness that would cure the discontentment for good.

Those God-given dreams for marriage turned into *"if only"* thoughts…

If only I had a boyfriend, then I would feel beautiful.
If only I were married, then I would feel happy.
If only I had a husband, then I would feel complete.

Have you ever thought *"if only"* thoughts like these?

Discontentment is defined as a "lack of satisfaction with one's possessions, status, or situation."

Based on this definition, it could be easy to think the cure to discontentment in our singleness would be to obtain a more satisfactory relationship status.

But the real danger of discontentment is that it's never satisfied. Once that greener grass on the other side is reached, we're left wanting even *greener* grass.

If we base our joy on fulfilled dreams, perfect circumstances and ideal situations, we'll keep being robbed of joy in our singleness, and even if we do get married, discontentment will follow us and cause a new batch of *"if only"* thoughts to steal our joy.

According to Scripture, we can have joy in all circumstances. In fact, as followers of Jesus, we're called to choose joy regardless of our circumstances and situations:

"Always be full of joy in the Lord. I say it again - rejoice!" Phil. 4:4

"Always be joyful. Never stop praying. Be thankful in all circumstances, for this is God's will for you who belong to Christ Jesus." 1 Thess. 5:16-18

"We can rejoice, too, when we run into problems and trials, for we know that they help us develop endurance." Rom. 5:3

"Dear brothers and sisters, when troubles of any kind come your way, consider it an opportunity for great joy." James 1:2

Joy is a gift of the Holy Spirit, the fruit of His work in our lives as we walk in step with Him. (See Gal. 5:16-25)

Joy is also a choice.

In our singleness, we can choose to grumble, complain, and think *"if only"* thoughts of discontentment.

Or we can choose to praise, give thanks, and rejoice.

Each of these actions is a declaration of our belief that God is good even in the not-so-good, that Jesus is enough even in our longings, that the Holy Spirit is an ever present help even in the hardest, scariest, saddest stuff.

Each of these actions is a declaration that singleness can't steal our joy, because our joy is found in Jesus.

Read Philippians 4:4-9.

What are we called to do in this passage?

What promises are given in this passage?

What types of "*if only*" thoughts do you think?

Brainstorm some ways you can intentionally give thanks and rejoice in the Lord, even on the hard days, then do it!

Day 20:

Where Are All the Good Guys?

I've said it, and I've heard many single women say it: *Where are all the good guys? There just aren't any good guys around here. All the good guys are already taken.*

I don't know about you, but when I say these things, it's usually with some hopelessness in my heart, and bit of whine in my voice.

In our singleness, we can tend to focus on what's missing and view our lives through a lens of lack.

We *aren't* married, we *don't* have a boyfriend, we're *not* going on dates, the dates we do go on *aren't* going anywhere, and there are *no good guys out there.*

In Matthew 6, Jesus is teaching His disciples about worry, specifically *not* to worry. And in this passage, He shifts their focus from what's lacking to what's right in front of them:

"Look at the birds. They don't plant or harvest or store food in barns, for your heavenly Father feeds them. And aren't you far more valuable to him than they are? Can all your worries add a single moment to your life?
"And why worry about your clothing? Look at the lilies of the field and how they grow. They don't work or make their clothing, yet Solomon in all his glory was not dressed as beautifully as they are. And if God cares so wonderfully for wildflowers that are here today and thrown into the fire tomorrow, he will certainly care for you. Why do you have so little faith?" (vv. 26-30)

Jesus encouraged His disciples to shift their focus and see the evidence all around them of God's provision, goodness, and care.

How much more joy would we have in our singleness if we were to shift our focus from what's lacking and missing, to the abundance and blessing of God's goodness right here, right now?

In this looking and noticing, our thoughts will go from worrisome thoughts - *What will we eat? What will we wear? Where are all the good guys? When will I ever get married?* - to trusting God and seeking Him.

I know it may not seem like it, and I know they can be hard to find, but there are good guys out there!

And, more importantly, there is a good God right here.

Read Matthew 6:25-34.

What reasons does Jesus give for not worrying? What does He tell us to do instead?

Do you tend to focus more on what you have or what you don't have?

Look around you. What evidence do you see of God's provision, goodness, and care in your right now life?

Day 21:

Caught in the Comparison Trap

I'm scrolling social media, laughing at the memes, liking the photos of my friends and family, and, let's be honest, wasting time watching all. the. tik. toks.

Somewhere in the middle of all this, I see an announcement that he popped the question and she said yes, accompanied by beautiful photos of smiling faces and a sparkling ring.

Why her and not me?
She's prettier, funnier, smarter.
She's happier, more popular, more successful.
I wish it would happen for me. I wish I had what she had.

Before I know it, I'm caught in the comparison trap, easy prey to discontentment.

As women, it's tempting to compare ourselves to other women, especially those who seem to have what we don't.

We've heard it said: *Comparison is the thief of joy.*

But really, comparison robs us of so much more: peace, compassion, patience, kindness, confidence, motivation, faith, creativity... all the good things of enjoying life, engaging with others, and experiencing God.

Comparison robs us of these blessings because it stirs up resentment, frustration, bitterness, doubts, worries, complacency, discouragement, and insecurities.

When we're caught up in comparison in our singleness, we're looking and longing for the blessings of what *she* has, whether that's a boyfriend, a better figure, or a bigger paycheck, rather than seeing and savoring the blessings God has already given us.

The enemy uses comparison to steal the gift of singleness by causing us to envy others. We're happy for our friends who are getting engaged, getting married, starting families, but maybe there's a small (or big) part of us that feels jealous. That thinks it's just not fair. That says we deserve this just as much as her. That resents her dreams coming true because ours aren't.

Scripture calls us to get rid of envy from our hearts. (See 1 Pet. 2:1)

We need to stop the comparing.

But how can we?

The opposite of envy is *generosity to others* and *being glad for others*.

Romans 12:13-15 says, "When God's people are in need, be ready to help them. Always be eager to practice hospitality. Bless those who persecute you. Don't curse them; pray that God will bless them. Be happy with those who are happy, and weep with those who weep."

Instead of looking at others through a lens of comparison, we are called to be compassionate. Instead of envying what someone else has, we are called to be generous with what we have.

We can do this by serving others, praying for others, being present with others, encouraging others, celebrating others.

As we do so, we'll make connections, discover purpose, build friendships, overcome challenges, and probably have a whole lot of fun along the way!

Read Romans 12:10-21.

According to this passage, what should our attitude be towards others?

How does comparison hinder us from having this attitude?

How would you see yourself and your singleness differently if you stopped comparing?

Brainstorm some ways you can cultivate gratitude, generosity, and compassion for others. Pick one of them to do this week (and maybe pick another to do next week!)

Day 22:

Who Said Your Life Has to Look Like That?

A 9-year-old girl once told me if I had gone to college, my chances of meeting Mr. Right would have increased, and I would probably be married by now.

Maybe she was right, but that wasn't the path for me.

Even though most women who go to college aren't going to look for a spouse, that tends to be the expectation for us.

What's the saying? *Ring by spring.*

There can be this pressure for our lives to follow a certain timeline: graduate, go to college, meet someone, date, get married, buy a home, start a family...

When life doesn't follow that timeline (and mine hasn't *at all*), we can feel like we're failing and falling behind.

But who said your life has to look like that?

Maybe it was a 9-year-old speaking from what she knew of her parents' story.
Maybe it's your aunt who married young and thinks you should, too.
Maybe it's the woman who was single and unhappy for a long time, and now she's finally married and wants the same happiness for you.
Maybe it's society's portrayal of romantic relationships as the ultimate fulfillment.
Maybe it's the pastor who uses marriage analogy after marriage analogy to describe our relationship with God.

There are these external pressures for our life to look a certain way. There are also internal pressures: my own desires and expectations, my comparing my life to another's, my envy of those who seem to be "on track", my thinking *if only* thoughts.

Do you remember those "I AM" statements we read on Days 1 and 5?

One of them was "I am the good shepherd." (Jn. 10:11)

In this passage where Jesus calls Himself the Good Shepherd, He calls us His sheep:

"The sheep recognize his voice and come to him. He calls his own sheep by name and leads them out... and they follow him because they know his voice." (vv. 3-4)

When it comes to how our lives should look, the One we need to be listening to is Jesus.

He will lead us. He will guide us. He will be our Good Shepherd.

And when we're following Him, the pressure is off.

Because following Jesus isn't about following a certain timeline or conforming to all the things we "should" be, but about following *Him* and being transformed into the women He created us to be.

So, we can be 30 (or 20-something or 40-something or 80-something) and still be single.

Because, ultimately, we don't want our lives to look like *that*. We want our lives to look like Jesus.

Read John 10:1-18.

How does Jesus describe the relationship between the good shepherd and his sheep?

When have you felt pressured that your life should look a certain way or follow a certain timeline?

What does following Jesus mean for you?

How does following Jesus take away the pressure of following certain timelines or expectations?

Day 23:

Don't Quit Your Daydream

Don't quit your daydream.

I've always liked that phrase. It reminds me to not take myself too seriously, keep a little whimsy in my day, and imagine the possibilities.

But sometimes, I imagine too many possibilities.

Have you ever met someone attractive and your mind automatically begins trying to determine if they're "the one?"

Have you ever gone on a first date and your mind jumps ahead to planning your future wedding?

Have you ever been at a holiday gathering, and your mind wanders what things would be like if you had a significant other to introduce to all your relatives?

Have you ever had a hard day and your mind plays out a romantic, heart-swelling scene of how it would have been different if you were only in a relationship?

It can be fun and good to envision the future and dream up possibilities.

But, if we're not careful, we can begin to live in our daydreams instead of being present to the life God has for us right now.

Hebrews 12:1-2 says, "Let us run with endurance the race God has set before us. We do this by keeping our eyes on Jesus, the champion who initiates and perfects our faith."

God has a race for us to run. Yes, He has good plans for our future, but I also believe He has good plans for our present.

There are gifts He is calling you to use, people He is leading you to serve, friendships He is giving you to enjoy, steps of faith He is inviting you to take, passions He is stirring in you to pursue.

But we can get so distracted by those daydreams, fixating on what *could be* or what *might have been*, instead of fixing our eyes on Jesus.

That's really what being present is all about: where our focus is.

Is our focus on Jesus: eyes open to His presence in our lives, attentive to His daily leading, alert to what would distract us from Him, seeing ourselves and others as He does, so we can engage in the life God has given us and run the race He has set before us?

Some days can be hard. Being single can be hard. And it can be tempting to daydream as an escape from the hard.

But when we escape from the hard, we also miss out on the joy, the beauty, the goodness, the work God is doing in it all.

So, don't quit your daydream.

But don't quit your right-now life either.

Don't quit being present for the life God has given you, the ways He is growing you, the people He has placed in front of you, the blessings He is pouring out to you, and the good work He is calling you to do in this moment.

Read Hebrews 12:1-4.

According to these verses, what must we do to run our race? What are we promised?

Do you ever daydream as a distraction from your singleness? What might it cause you to miss out on?

What would it look like for you to be present and run your race?

Day 24:
You Can Have Both

Being content in our singleness doesn't mean we can't desire marriage.

Let me say it again: you can have contentment in singleness *and* have a desire for marriage.

You can have both.

I say it multiple times because, if you're anything like me, you might have gotten this idea in your head that you *can't* have both.

You might have even gotten this idea in your head that only when you're perfectly happy being single and have no longings whatsoever for marriage, that's when you'll meet your person.

In this thinking, we'll find ourselves trying to trick God.

We'll try to manufacture contentment, covering up our longings and hiding away our dreams, so God will give us our heart's desires.

But that defeats the purpose of what contentment is all about.

Because contentment isn't about being happy so that we'll get what we want, and it isn't about being happy because we have what we want.

In Philippians 4:12, Paul writes, "I know what it is to be in need, and I know what it is to have plenty. I have learned the secret of being content in any and every situation." (NIV)

Lest we think Paul's life was all roses and cupcakes, here's a bit of his backstory: after going from persecuting Christians to being a follower of Jesus, Paul began to start churches. While he was doing this, he was thrown in prison several times, was beaten, stoned, shipwrecked, and on occasion went without food. (2 Cor. 11:23-27) At the time of writing Philippians 4, he was under house arrest, with the possibility of being executed for his faith (which he eventually was).

Paul *learned* to be content. This means contentment doesn't automatically come when we have plenty. It also means we can have wants and needs, and still be content.

How?

One of the most popular verses in the Bible tells us: "I can do all things through Christ who strengthens me." (Phil. 4:13, NKJV)

The word "content" used in Philippians 4 comes from the Greek word *autarkes*. It means "sufficient, adequate, needing no assistance."

The word "strengthens" comes from the Greek word *arkeo*, which means "to have sufficient strength, to be enough for a thing."

Paul is saying that in Christ, he has all he needs to do whatever he is called to do, regardless of the circumstances. In Christ, he is already able, adequate, and enough.

So being content in our singleness doesn't mean being perfectly happy and not having longings. It means in both want and plenty, in both happiness and longings, in both singleness and marriage, we have strength and sufficiency in Christ to be the women He created us to be and live the lives He calls us to live.

Read Philippians 4:11-13.

Do you see singleness as being "in want" or "in plenty"? Do you think it has to be one or the other, or can it be both?

Have you ever tried to be content so God would bring you a spouse? How did that make you feel about yourself, your singleness, your relationship with God?

List all the ways Jesus strengthens (*arkeo*) you.

Part 5:

Single On Purpose

Day 25:

All the Single Ladies... in Scripture

Miriam, Zelophehad's daughters, Rahab, Ruth, Anna, Martha, Mary of Bethany, Mary Magdalene...

What do all these women have in common?

Besides all being in the Bible, when we meet each one in Scripture, they're single.

They're single in a time and culture when singleness could be seen as disgraceful, and even dangerous, for a woman.

But their singleness didn't stop them from doing some incredible things.

Miriam watched over her baby brother as he came into Pharaoh's daughter's care. Years later, she led the people in worship as they left Egypt and helped that same brother lead the nation of Israel on their way to the Promised Land. (Ex. 2:1-10, 15:20-21)

Zelophehad's daughters spoke up for their inheritance after their father's death and, as a result of their boldness, God gave the Israelites a new law that would provide for future generations of women who found themselves in similar circumstances. (Num. 27:1-11)

Rahab would eventually marry and become one of five women named in Jesus' genealogy, but before that she risked her life to help Israelite spies because she feared the Lord. (Josh. 2:1-21, 6:17; Matt. 1:5)

Ruth was a widow who would eventually marry again and also be included in Jesus' genealogy, but during her singleness, she chose to leave the familiarity and security of her homeland to care for her widowed mother-in-law. (Ruth 1-4; Matthew 1:5)

Anna was married only seven years, then lived as a prophet, staying at the temple to worship, fast, and pray. When she saw baby Jesus, she recognized He was the Messiah, and spoke about Him to others. (Lk. 2:36-38)

Martha was a friend of Jesus, regularly opening her home to Him during His ministry. She witnessed Him raising her brother back to life, and it was to her that Jesus declared the words, "I am the resurrection and the life." (Lk. 10:38-42; Jn. 11:1-44)

Mary of Bethany (Martha's sister) defied cultural expectations to sit at Jesus' feet and listen to His teaching, for which He commended her. On another occasion, Jesus again commended her for her act of worship in anointing His feet with oil. And she too witnessed Jesus raising her brother to life. (Lk. 10:38-42; Jn. 11:1-44, 12:1-8)

Mary Magdalene, after being freed from seven demons, supported Jesus in His ministry. She was entrusted to be the first witness of the resurrected Christ, and to tell Jesus' disciples that He was alive. (Lk. 8:1-3; Jn. 20:1-18)

Friend, you're in good company!

No, these women weren't perfect. But they each encountered God's saving grace, experienced His transforming love, and were empowered by His Spirit to do what He had called them to do.

God is not limited by your relationship status. So don't limit yourself.

If He could use these women in their singleness to lead nations, shape laws, save lives, care for widows, speak truth, support others, and spread the gospel, just imagine what He could do through you as you live surrendered and obedient to Him.

Which of these women do you relate most to? Why?

Using the passages listed above, pick one of these women's stories to read. How does her story encourage you? What do you learn about God? About His purpose for His daughters? About yourself?

Day 26:

Single on Purpose

I've been single all my life. As I shared before, in my early twenties I wasn't happy about that.

Not only did I feel discontent, I also felt purposeless.

But that wasn't because I didn't have purpose in my singleness, but because I wasn't living purposefully in my singleness.

What if we were to be single on purpose?

This doesn't mean we no longer want to be married or are choosing to be single forever.

Rather, it means choosing to live in our singleness with purpose and intentionality, instead of in default mode or "in the meantime."

Back on Day 6, we read in Genesis 1 how we are created in the image of God, made for relationship with Him and to reflect Him in our relationships with others.

After God created man and woman in His image, He blessed them:

"Be fruitful and multiply. Fill the earth and govern it. Reign over the fish in the sea, the birds in the sky, and all the animals that scurry along the ground." (Gen. 1:28)

God created people in His image and then He blessed them with purpose and mission. He gave them work to do, a responsibility to steward that image in which they were created and care for the world around them.

The phrase "be fruitful" isn't just talking about having babies. The literal translation from the Hebrew word *parah* is "bear fruit." It speaks of being productive, doing good work, creating and cultivating.

In Galatians 5:22-23, we read about the fruit of the Spirit: love, joy, peace, patience, kindness, goodness, faithfulness, gentleness, and self-control.

There are many other places in Scripture where similar characteristics are listed as ones we as followers of Jesus are to have.

Really, these characteristics, this fruit, are about having Christ-like character. We are to become more and more like Jesus.

In the verses surrounding the fruit of the Spirit, we are called to "walk by the Spirit" and "keep in step with the Spirit." (vv. 16 and 25, NIV)

We bear this fruit of Christ-likeness by submitting to and engaging in the work the Holy Spirit is doing in our lives: confessing sin, getting into God's Word, praying, participating in godly community.

In our singleness, who are we becoming? What are we cultivating? What are we doing on purpose?

In Christ, our singleness can be fruitful. It doesn't have to be a default mode. It can be a time in which we actively and purposefully become more and more the women God created us to be.

Being single on purpose doesn't mean we choose to be single forever, but it does mean we choose to cultivate, grow, and bear the fruit of Christ-likeness.

Read John 15:1-8.

According to this passage, how is fruit produced?

What does being single on purpose mean for you?

What things are you cultivating in this season of singleness?

How could you steward your singleness to bear fruit?

Day 27:

Share the Gift

Your singleness is a gift.

In Scripture, the blessings and gifts God gives are meant to be shared. They are meant to be a blessing and gift not just for ourselves, but for others as well.

I really didn't think about my singleness being a gift I could share until my nieces were born.

I realized I wanted to be an aunt who helped these precious girls know their identity, worth, and significance are found in Christ alone... not boyfriends or popularity or pretty faces.

But I also realized this would be hard to do if I didn't believe it for myself.

My journey of becoming content and confident in my singleness is no longer just for myself.

It's also for my nieces and nephews. For my friends. For my little sisters. For the young girls and boys at my church. These are all people God has placed in my life to whom I can be a blessing and example.

Yesterday, we read God's blessing to man and woman in Genesis 1:

"Be fruitful and multiply. Fill the earth and govern it. Reign over the fish in the sea, the birds in the sky, and all the animals that scurry along the ground." (v. 28)

God blesses, and then He tells them to be a blessing to the world around them.

The word "multiply" in this verse speaks of discipleship.

When Jesus began His ministry on earth, He called men to follow Him:

"Come, follow me, and I will show you how to fish for people!" (Matt. 4:19)

Jesus invited these fishermen to be His disciples: to learn from Him, to imitate Him, to become like Him.

After they had followed Him for three years and before He returned to heaven, Jesus gave them this mission:

"Go and make disciples of all the nations, baptizing them in the name of the Father and the Son and the Holy Spirit. Teach these new disciples to obey all the commands I have given you." (Matt. 28:19-20)

There's a question I heard often growing up in church: Who are you discipling, and who's discipling you?

How we live our singleness will impact how we disciple others.

Because our singleness will tell a story. Either a story that says we need a significant other to be complete and happy, we don't have real purpose until we're married, or we're not good enough until we have a ring on our finger.

Or it could tell the story of the Gospel: our worth is found in Jesus, we are made complete and whole and good enough through His sacrifice, and in relationship with Him, we can live a life full of purpose, joy, peace, and hope.

Read Matthew 28:18-20 and Acts 1:6-10.

What does Jesus call us to do in these verses? What promises are given?

Who has been an example to you of full life in Jesus?

Who has God placed in your life to whom you can be an example?

What story is your singleness telling to those around you? Is it the story you want it to tell?

Day 28:
Greater Love

Where are you looking for love? Where are you leaning in close to hear the whispered, *I love you*?

We can so often look at marriage, romance, boy meets girl, as the highest form of love and relationship.

But Scripture tells us a different love story in its use of the word "love."

In the Greek language in which most of the New Testament was written, there are four different words for love:

Eros is the word used to describe romantic love.
Philia is the word used to describe brotherly-sisterly love between peers.
Storge is the word used to describe a parent's love for a child.
And *agape* is the word for the love of God. It describes the love of the Trinity: whole, holy, and selfless love. This is the love that created us and works in us and through us to enable us to love God and love others as He does.

In the New Testament, *agape* is used 249 times. Next is *philia*, used only 54 times.

Want to know how many times *eros* and *storge* are used?

Zero.

I know, I was surprised too.

Even in places where instructions are given about marriage and parenting, it is not the word *eros* or *storge*, but *agape* that is used. As

Christ-followers, this is the love we are to be walking in, displaying, and sharing in all our relationships.

This is the love that God pours out to us, this is the love that transforms us in Christ-likeness, and this is the love we can pour out to others in our relationships with them.

What does this love look like lived out?

In a word: *Jesus*.

In John 15, Jesus says, "There is no greater love than to lay down one's life for one's friends." (v. 13)

Maybe when we read this verse, our minds recall Jesus' sacrifice. This was an act of love. First, love between the Father and the Son, so deep and sure that Jesus would trust and obey, even to death.

Then, love for us, to redeem us from sin and separation and restore us in relationship with God, and in relationship with others.

That's a beautiful thing about the Gospel: it brings what was separated together.

We who were enemies of God are now called His friends. And we who were divided by culture and nationality, age and generation, social and economic status, are now brought together in unity of faith and friendship.

Romance isn't a bad thing. But it is not the ultimate form of love.

There is a greater love: the love of God to us, in us, and through us, deepening our trust, transforming our character, motivating our obedience, and compelling us to serve others in Christ-like love.

Read John 15:9-17.

What does Jesus promise in this passage? How does He call us to live?

Have you viewed marriage and romance as the ultimate forms of love and relationship?

Spend some time thanking God for the different relationships He has given you in which you can experience and express His love.

Day 29:

For the Days You're Discouraged

Can I be honest with you?

All the words I've written in this devotional are words my own heart needs as well.

Even though I've grown a lot in contentment in my singleness, there are still days I'm discouraged.

There are still days I ask, *When will I ever get married?* There are still days I wonder why my dreams aren't coming true, still days I compare and complain, still days I feel lonely and insecure in my singleness.

You're probably still going to experience those days, too.

Maybe a date doesn't go as hoped, or you're not even getting opportunities to go on dates. Maybe another holiday season comes around and you're still waiting under the mistletoe by yourself. Maybe a well-meaning co-worker or relative or someone at church asks one of those awkward questions or makes one of those insensitive comments about you being single and it leaves you feeling *bleh.*

There are going to be days we feel discouraged, wanting to cry or scream or vent our frustration.

And that's okay. It doesn't mean we're somehow not a good Christian or that we love Jesus less.

There's a whole book in the Bible that is full of emotions and feelings and raw, honest, vulnerable pouring out of the heart.

It's the book of Psalms:

"Why am I discouraged?
   Why is my heart so sad?
I will put my hope in God!
   I will praise him again -
   my Savior and my God!" Ps. 42:5-6

On the days you're discouraged, ask yourself why. Is it loneliness? Something someone said? Comparing yourself to someone else? Worrying about the future? An insecurity gripping your heart?

Acknowledge these feelings and confess them to Jesus. Put your hope in Him.

There's something else the book of Psalms is full of: declarations of who God is, how even in the scariest, hardest, messiest, saddest of circumstances, He is still worthy of praise, because He is still our Savior.

There are going to be days when we feel discouraged, but I believe as we walk with Jesus, there will be more days when we are encouraged.

When we sense His presence amidst the loneliness.
When we hear His voice speaking to our hearts over the confusion and insecurities.
When we experience His healing and comfort in the heartache.
When we have peace knowing He holds our future and has the best of plans for us.
When we are filled with joy because of His goodness to us.
When we are empowered by the truth of His love for us.

So on the days you're discouraged, pour out your heart to Jesus and let yourself be encouraged by Him.

Pick a Psalm to read. It can be a favorite of yours, or one you've never read before. (If picking a random Psalm to read feels overwhelming, here are a few of my favorites: Psalm 23, Psalm 42, Psalm 130.)

What emotions are expressed in this Psalm?

What does this Psalm say about God?

When was a time you were discouraged and then experienced encouragement?

Do you feel like you can be honest with God with your feelings about your singleness? Let's try: write a prayer confessing your honest feelings to God. Then sit with Him, allowing Him to speak to your heart.

Day 30:

The Next Chapter

Would you believe me if I said I'm a little teary-eyed as I write these words to you?

Because I'm still just so overjoyed, humbled, and expectant that you're reading this.

Overjoyed that you've journeyed to this final day of learning to see yourself and your singleness as Jesus does, humbled that my words may have helped you in some way, and expectant that God is going to continue His beautiful, powerful, transformational work in your heart.

Because even though we've come to the last day of this devotional, this isn't the end.

This is the point where we make a choice: are we going to go back to the old way of thinking and living in our singleness, or are we going to continue to see ourselves and our singleness as Jesus does, and live with joy and confidence in Him?

In Philippians 1, Paul (yep, him again!), writes these words to the believers in Philippi:

"And I am certain that God, who began the good work within you, will continue his work until it is finally finished on the day when Christ Jesus returns." (v. 6)

I'm certain of this for you as well. God will continue His good work in you, not just in your singleness, but in every struggle, every insecurity, every adventure, every worry, every dream, every disappointment, every heartache, every step of faith, every area of your life.

So even though this is the end, it's also a beginning. The start of another chapter in the story God is writing for your good and for His glory. The next step in your journey with your Lord, Savior, and Friend, Jesus.

Let's take some time to reflect on the last 30 days, and then look forward to the next chapter:

How have you grown throughout the last 30 days? What has God taught you? What encouraged you?

Look back at your answer on Day 1 to the question *What does singleness mean to you?* What does it mean now? How has your perspective/thinking/attitude changed?

What is the next step in seeing yourself and your singleness as Jesus does?

What is one thing you can do to apply what you have learned?

Acknowledgements

Even though I'm always writing by myself in my room, I'm not alone in bringing those words into the world for readers. And there's no way I would be able to if I was. There are so many people who have encouraged, supported, and helped me in different ways throughout the writing process.

A big thanks and even bigger hug to my family, and especially to my mom and sisters, for being sounding boards for my ideas, providing early feedback on everything from content to cover design, and for putting up with random text messages when I can't seem to make a decision.

Thank you to Mammaw for using your grammatical skills to edit my spelling and punctuation and make this devotional as read-able as possible.

To my friends in Hope*Writers, especially those in the Self-Publishing and Single Writers Hope*Circles, your encouragement, feedback, and advice has been invaluable.

Of course, I have to thank YOU, dear reader, for reading these words of mine and supporting me through purchases, emails, follows, and likes. You're the reason I write.

And finally, I give thanks and praise to my Lord and Savior Jesus Christ, who has given this single girl abiding joy, calming peace, and inspiring hope for this season, and for always. All glory be to You.

About the Author

Jessica Faith Hagen is a writer and speaker who shares biblical encouragement and practical advice to help women know their worth in Christ, navigate singleness with joy, and live wholeheartedly for Jesus. She is the author of *Come: A Journaling Journey Through the Life of Jesus* and *Wonderful: A Devotional Journal for the Christmas Season*. Find more encouragement and connect with Jessica online @jessicafaithwrites and on her website theoverflowing.com.

Bibliography

Arthur, Kay. *Discover the Bible for Yourself.* Harvest House Publishers, 2000

Arthur, Kay. *Lord, I Want to Know You: a Devotional Study of the Names of God.* Multnomah Books, 1992

The Wesleyan Bible Commentary, by Charles W. Carter et al., vol. 1, part 1, William B. Eerdmans Publishing Company, 1967

"Discontent." *Merriam-Webster.com Dictionary*, Merriam-Webster, https://www.merriam-webster.com/dictionary/discontent. Accessed 12 Nov. 2020.

Erdman, Charles R. *An Exposition: The First Epistle of Paul to the Corinthians.* The Westminster Press, 1998

The Expositor's Bible Commentary. with the New International Version of the Holy Bible, by Frank E. Gaebelein et al., vol. 10, Zondervan Pub. House, 1976.

Piper, John. "Battling the Unbelief of Envy" *Desiring God*, 1988, https://www.desiringgod.org/messages/battling-the-unbelief-of-envy

Piper, John. "'I Am Who I Am'." *Desiring God*, 1984, https://www.desiringgod.org/messages/i-am-who-i-am

Strong, James. *The New Strong's Expanded Exhaustive Concordance of the Bible.* Thomas Nelson Publishers, 2010

"What is the opposite of envy?" *WordHippo.com Thesaurus*, Word Hippo, https://www.wordhippo.com/what-is/the-opposite-of/envy.html. Accessed 19 Nov. 2020

Wilkin, Jen. *In His Image: 10 ways God calls us to reflect his character.* Crossway, 2018